Fathers, Children, and the Intergenerational Transmission of Employers*

Martha Stinson and Christopher Wignall[†]

April 30, 2014

Abstract

We document the tendency of fathers in the U.S. to share employers with their sons and daughters. We show that the incidence of sharing employers is much higher than can be explained by the fact that fathers and sons tend to live near each other. Workers early in their careers are much more likely to share their father's employer, as are children of high-earning fathers. We find that children's earnings at shared employers tend to be higher than at unshared jobs, especially for children of high-earning fathers. These facts indicate that employer sharing between fathers and children could explain some component of the intergenerational elasticity of earnings in the United States.

1 Introduction

The sharing of employers by parents and children is a phenomenon often thought to be a means whereby a parent helps a child's successful transition into the labor market. However, the extent to which children go to work for firms which employ their parents has not been widely studied and never with U.S. data. In this paper, we seek to fill that gap by providing a thorough documentation of the tendency of children to find jobs with their fathers' employers, including an evaluation of the characteristics that predict the likelihood of such employer sharing. Based on a sample of sons from a Census Bureau survey, we show that in the U.S. in 2010, 9.6% of working sons from a home where a father

---

*Any views expressed on statistical, methodological, technical, or operational issues are those of the authors and not necessarily those of the U.S. Census Bureau. All data used in this paper are confidential. Estimates are calculated without sample weights, and so are not nationally representative. Calculated standard errors do not account for the SIPP sample design. The estimates in this paper are based on responses from a sample of the population. As with all surveys, estimates may vary from the actual values because of sampling variation and other factors. All comparisons made in this paper have undergone statistical testing and are significant at the 95-percent confidence level unless otherwise noted.

[†]Stinson: U.S. Census Bureau, 4600 Silver Hill Rd, Washington, DC 20233, martha.stinson@census.gov. Wignall: U.S. Census Bureau, 4600 Silver Hill Rd, Washington, DC 20233, christopher.d.wignall@census.gov.

was present in the son's teenage years shared an employer with that father. Approximately 22% of sons will simultaneously share an employer with their father by the time they reach age 30. An additional 6% of sons will work at an employer that previously employed their father, although the father left before the son began his employment. Approximately 13% of daughters work simultaneously with their father at an employer at some point by age 30, and another 4% work at for a former employer of their father. For both sons and daughters, jobs are more likely to be shared with fathers when the child is young (under 18). The tendency to share an employer is also related to the father's earnings, with higher-earning fathers more likely to share employers with their sons and daughters.

We also investigate the relationship between this intergenerational transmission of employers and children's labor market outcomes. With only controls for age, tenure, and overall labor force experience, we initially find that sharing an employer is correlated with higher earnings for the son. This is true for jobs in general and particularly for the son's first job and highest earning job at age 30. We find that this relationship between earnings and job sharing is stronger for sons of higher-earning fathers. However when we control for employer characteristics such as industry and firm size, we find that, for most NAICS sectors, sharing an employer does not give sons an earnings advantage relative to others in the same industry. Employer sector is a predictor of shared employment, with jobs in the manufacturing and construction sectors more likely to be shared than jobs in the scientific, professional, and technical sector. Daughters' earnings, on the other hand, are not generally higher in shared jobs.

The tendency of children to find jobs with their fathers' employers is related to two important economic issues: intergenerational economic mobility and the role of social networks in job search. First, the prevalence of fathers and sons sharing employers provides an additional plausible explanation for the high correlation between fathers' and sons' earnings. A substantial literature has analyzed the intergenerational elasticity of earnings and established the low intergenerational economic mobility in the U.S. relative to Western European countries.[1] The most common explanations for the correlation between fathers' and sons' earnings are heritability of ability and parental investment in children's human capital. But the intergenerational transmission of employers could also explain the intergenerational transmission of earnings. If fathers benefit their sons by helping them find jobs with the father's own employer, and high-earning fathers are more likely to thus help their sons, then high-earning fathers are more likely to have high-earning sons. Similarly, fathers with a weak attachment to the labor force (and, consequently, low earnings) may be less able to help their sons find employment, and so will be more likely to have sons who also have low earnings. Furthermore, the benefit to a son of sharing an employer with his father may depend on the characteristics of the employer. For example, a high-earning father's employer may tend to pay higher wages than a low-earning father's employer, so that the son of the high-earning father

---

[1] See Black and Devereaux (2010) for a thorough survey of this literature.

tends to benefit more from sharing employers. Even at the same employer, a high-earning father may be able to secure his son a better job (e.g. higher wage or more prestigious) than a lower-earning coworker can secure for his own son. While our data do not allow us to confidently estimate causal effects, most of our evidence is consistent with the former hypothesis. Fathers are able to get their sons better jobs than they otherwise would on their own but do not generally seem to provide them higher earnings than others in the same industry, for example.

Second, the tendency of children to find jobs at their fathers' employers adds to the understanding of the role of social networks in job search. Several recent papers have highlighted the importance of interpersonal relationships in finding jobs and have evaluated the benefits to employers and employees from using a social network to improve job matches. Our work seeks to demonstrate the existence and influence of a family network and to show how this network might aid children throughout their early work history.

We caution that our measured relationships cannot be interpreted as a casual effect of sharing an employer on children's earnings. The father's decision to assist his child in finding an employer, the child's decision to seek and accept a job with his or her father's employer, and the employer's decision to hire its employee's child are all likely to be correlated with important unobserved determinants of the child's labor-force outcomes. For example, if fathers tend to help their most capable children, seeing in them the highest potential for benefit from job-search assistance, then any evidence of higher earnings due to sharing an employer may simply be due to these children's higher ability. The converse may also be true if fathers help their troubled children, feeling that without intervention these children may have adverse labor market outcomes. In this case, the effect will be biased downwards. Without adequately controlling for all characteristics of the child, it is hard to establish causality between shared employer and earnings outcomes.[2] In spite of our estimate of the relationship between intergenerational transmission of employers and transmission of earnings not being casual, we believe that these results are an important first step in documenting the existence and importance of parent-child networks in the U.S. labor market and provide a useful starting point for further research on the social implications of this employment pattern.

2 Background

Previous research on shared employment between fathers and children is relatively limited and has used only Scandinavian and Canadian data. Kramarz and Skans (2010, Swedish data), Corak and Piraino (2011, Canadian data), and

---

[2] An example of an analysis that could identify a casual effect would compare one group of sons whose fathers' work circumstances prohibit shared employment to another group of sons whose fathers face no such restriction, and where this restriction is unrelated to sons' and fathers' unobserved characteristics. We are not aware of any U.S. data that could be used for this type of analysis.

Bingley, Corak, and Westergard-Nielsen (2012, Canadian and Danish data) all calculate the percentage of some group of fathers and sons who share employers and investigate the how shared employers are related to sons' labor-market outcomes. Corak and Piraino (2011) and Bingley, Corak, and Westergard-Nielsen (2012) calculate that by the time a son has reached his early thirties, the likelihood he has worked for an employer that also employed his father at some point is 28% for Danes and 40% for Canadians. Similarly, when the son is 30, the likelihood that his main employer is the same as the main employer of his father when the son was a teenager is 4% in Denmark and 5.6% in Canada. Kramarz and Skans report that in Sweden in 2002, just under 8% of employed fathers with employed children shared an employer.

These estimates are remarkably similar to our estimates of the percentage of sons sharing employers with their fathers in 2010 (9.6%) and the percentage of sons who by age 30 had worked at an employer who had also employed their fathers at some point (28%). This similarity is surprising given several reasons one might expect the phenomenon of intergenerational transmission of employers to be different in the U.S. than Canada or Scandinavia. As relatively small countries, one might suppose that both Denmark and Sweden would have a higher prevalence of shared parent-child employers simply due to the smaller number of employers overall. While Canada is a large country geographically, its labor market is much smaller than the U.S. and, due to language and population density differences, is probably more segmented. This again might lead to higher rates of shared employers among family members. U.S. families may be more geographically mobile and children and parents may live further apart on average than parents and children in Scandinavia or Canada, again contributing to a lower rate of shared employers in the U.S. relative to these countries. In contrast, the measured intergenerational elasticity of earnings in the U.S. is much higher than in these countries,[3] which may indicate a stronger relationship between fathers' and children's labor-force outcomes in the U.S. Because of the (potentially countervailing) effects of these differences between the U.S. labor market and those previously studied, our analysis provides a useful addition to the literature by showing that family networks are similarly important in the U.S. labor market.

Some previous related research using U.S. data does exist. Perez-Gonzalez (2006) is a closely related analysis showing that new CEOs are often the children of previous CEOs or of large shareholders. Other research, such as Hellerstein and Morrill (2008), has shown that fathers and sons tend to have the same occupations. However, this paper is the first documentation of the extent to which sons and daughters in the U.S. get jobs with their fathers' employers.

While all three of the father-child employer papers cited above calculate the percentage of shared employers, Kramarz and Skans (2010) approach the problem from the viewpoint of social networks. As the authors point out, one of the largest challenges in the network literature is establishing the existence of a network since researchers are often forced to define the network based on

---

[3] See, for example, Jantti (2006)

shared characteristics, such as residential location. In contrast, they suggest, family relationships are relatively easy to identify and hence the proof of the existence of a network hinges mainly on whether the family relationship produces different outcomes than would otherwise be expected. Kramarz and Skans's main contribution is demonstrating that family relationships do influence labor market outcomes in the Swedish labor market in a way that persuasively documents the family network existence. They use extensive administrative data on young Swedish adults graduating from school and obtaining their first jobs to investigate how often children end up at the same firms as their parents. Due to the universal coverage of their data, they are able to estimate the fraction of graduating students hired by a particular plant who also have parents working at that plant and the fraction of graduating students hired who do not have parents working at that plant. The difference between these two percentages is an estimate of the importance of family networks in the hiring process. They find that graduating children are 3%–10% more likely to work for a plant that employs their father than classmates without a parent at the plant.

In contrast, Corak and Piraino (2011) and Bingley, Corak, and Westergard-Nielsen (2012) focus mainly on analyzing the relationship between shared employment and the intergenerational transfer of economic advantage. They show that the intergenerational correlation between father and son permanent earnings is higher when a main employer is shared and hence point to common employers as a mechanism for creating intergenerational correlation in income. They particularly emphasize that shared employment is more common among the highest-earning fathers and show that, in Canada, the interaction between sharing an employer and father's permanent income is more highly correlated with the son's permanent income when the father is in the top decile of the earnings distribution than if the father is in the bottom decile. While Kramarz and Skans also investigate outcomes for children who share employers with their parents, their analysis is restricted to the impact at the first job after graduating from school. They find an adverse effect on initial wages but an increase in the length of time spent with the employer. They also report results that speak to the existence of a selection bias: in the Swedish labor market, it is the educationally low-achieving sons who are more likely to share employers. This may help explain the finding of lower initial son wages at shared employers. But their analysis does not further explore the long-run effects of sharing a first employer nor do they consider shared employment in an intergenerational correlation framework.

Our paper seeks to bring these two strands of the literature together by both documenting the existence of a family social network in the U.S. labor market and by showing how the existence of an influential network is correlated with the transmission of economic outcomes from fathers to sons. First, we extend the analyses of Corak and Piraino (2011) and Bingley, Corak, and Westergard-Nielsen (2012) to establish that the prevalence of the intergenerational transmission of employers in the U.S. is higher than can be explained by fathers' and sons' characteristics, such as residential location. Since, for example, sons are likely to live near their fathers, some fathers and sons will share employers simply because of the finite number of employers in the local labor market. We show that a father is much more likely to share an employer with his son than with an unrelated man who is otherwise very similar to his son.

Second, as is done to some extent in all three papers, we provide a detailed analysis of the determinants of fathers and children sharing employers. Similar to Corak and Piraino (2011), we find that the highest-earning fathers are more likely to share employers with their children, both sons and daughters. In contrast to them, however, we find that the lowest-earning fathers are the least likely to share employers. We also establish that children are most likely to share employers in their teens, with the probability of sharing decreasing monotonically as they age. We expand these analyses to investigate how the probability of sharing jobs is correlated with other characteristics, such as race and education of the father.

Finally, this paper expands on previous analyses of the relationship between job sharing and children's earnings by examining outcomes beyond just the first job or the shared job. Using a long administrative earnings history, we follow children from their first job in the formal labor market until their early thirties and identify shared employers at any point during this history. We are thus able to estimate the relationship between shared employment and children's earnings at their first job (like Kramarz and Skans), at their jobs at age 30 (like Corak and Piraino), and at all jobs in between.

3 Data

To answer questions about shared employment between fathers and children we require data that links parents and children to each other and to their respective employers. In order to determine whether the rate of shared employment is higher than mere chance would dictate, we need data that links all other workers of the same gender and age as our sample to their employers. Finally in order to condition on geography, we need data that assigns workers to residence locations. We assemble all these pieces using several Census Bureau data sets linked to administrative data. Unfortunately at this point in time, our results using these data are limited to sons only but we hope to add daughters to this portion of our analysis in the near future.

We begin with the Survey of Income and Program Participation which connects fathers and sons and provides SSNs to link all family members to administrative data.[4] Using nine SIPP panels, conducted between 1984 and 2008, we select sons who were 17 years or younger at the time of their SIPP panel and at least 15 years old by 2010, linked to their fathers,[5] and both father and son

---

[4]For the 1984, 1990, 1991, 1992, 1993, 1996, and 2001 panels, SIPP respondents were asked to provide their social security numbers, which were then validated by the U.S. Census Bureau in conjunction with the Social Security Administration. Since the 2004 panel, the Census Bureau has used a probabilistic matching process to assign Social Security Numbers to SIPP respondents. This process uses respondent-provided demographic information, such as gender and date of birth.

[5]This analysis includes all types of fathers: biological, step, and adopted. Future work will

had SSNs which linked to administrative data. These selection criteria give us a sample of 35,454 sons between the ages of 15 and 43 in 2010 with 26,761 unique fathers. These sons and fathers then link to a W-2 Universe File which includes all employees in the United States in 2010 whose employers were required to file W-2 reports with the IRS. To this W-2 Universe File we add information about gender and birthdate from the SSA Numident File. This combined file gives us employment information about both our sample of sons and fathers and all other men ages 15-43 in 2010. We use the Census Master Address File (MAF) and a crosswalk that links individuals to a given address for a particular year in order to determine residence location for our sons and all other working males in the appropriate age range. Our final sample of sons who have jobs reported in the W-2 data for 2010, match to an address in the MAF for 2010, match to the Numident, and have fathers who match to the W-2 data for 2010 is 16,487. These sons have 13,082 unique fathers. Table 1 shows the steps of the linking process and reports the sample size after each step. Our largest loss of sample comes from dropping fathers who had no W-2 employment in 2010. Table 2 shows the status of these non-employed fathers as far as can be determined from other administrative data sources. Over 40% are receiving Social Security retirement or disability payments, another 19% are self-employed, and 33% are unemployed, out of the labor market, or working in the informal sector and not receiving W-2s. We drop these fathers because by definition they cannot share an employer with their sons in 2010. Thus our calculations about percentages of fathers and sons who share employers should be interpreted as the percentage of working sons and fathers.

Because of the structure of this SIPP data (using several panels over a long period of time), standard survey weights are not appropriate. Thus, we do not have a nationally representative sample, and all our analyses represent an evaluation of the particular sample for which we have data.

The second part of our analysis relies on a link between the SIPP and the Detailed Earnings Record (DER) Extract from the Social Security Administration's Master Earnings File (MEF). The DER provides a history of earnings by employer from 1978 to 2011. From this source we are able to determine whether children and fathers have ever shared an employer and we are able to look across children's entire earnings histories and measure correlations between shared employment and earnings outcomes at the same and different points in time. Our sample of SIPP respondents is slightly different for this section of our paper because we require children who are old enough to have adult outcomes. Thus we limit ourselves to SIPP children who match to their fathers, were no older than 17 at the time of the survey, had SSNs and fathers with SSNs, and who were at least 30 years old by 2011, giving us a sample of 9,503 sons matched to 7,952 fathers and 8,458 daughters matched to 7,290 fathers.[6] We then restrict our sample to children who had DER earnings histories that included at least one

---

split the analysis based on type of father.

[6]This sample only uses sons from the 1984, 1990, 1991, 1992, 1993, and 1996 SIPP panels because sons who were 17 or under when they were surveyed in the 2000s decade did not turn 30 years old by 2010.

regular employer (i.e. we dropped individuals who either had no work history or only self-employment) and who had fathers with DER earnings histories. Table 3 shows the steps of this linking process and the number of observations in the son and daughter samples at each stage.

All of our analyses focus on whether a child ever had a job with the same employer as his or her father, simultaneously with his or her father, and starting subsequent to his or her father. In other words, our definition of a shared employer requires that the father began working at the employer before the child did and the child began working at the employer before the father stopped working at that employer. We thereby categorize each of the children's jobs as either shared or unshared.

We define employers based on the Employer Identification Number, which is a unique identifier assigned by the IRS to each employer in the U.S. We define a job as a spell at an employer. Importantly, the EIN is assigned to each employer, not to each establishment. Therefore, a father and child who work at different establishments of a single employer are considered to share an employer. Similarly, a transition from one establishment to another within the same employer is considered a continuation of the same job because we are unable to see any indication of such transitions in the data. We obtain firm characteristics by using the EIN as a linking identifier between the DER data and the Census Business Register (BR), the master list of all businesses operating in the United States, maintained by the Census Bureau as the sampling frame for firm-level surveys. Hence, the W-2 records provide the history of where the fathers and children worked, and the Business Register provides characteristics of those employers including industry, firm size, and whether the firm was a multi- or single unit business.

Industry classification changes over time, both due to changes in what the firm produces and also due to changes in standard industry codes. During the time period covered by our data (1978-2011), the United States switched from the Standard Industrial Classification (SIC) system the to North American Industrial Classification System (NAICS) as the official industry classification system. Thus, in order to accurately assign firms to industries, we use a longitudinally edited form of the BR called the Longitudinal Business Database (LBD). This file contains a 2007 NAICS code for most establishment-year pairs.

There are some W-2 jobs that do not match to the LBD. For these cases, we try to match to the annual Business Register files. If matching to the Business Register is successful, we then convert the reported industry to a 2007 NAICS code using our own approximate crosswalk of major SIC and NAICS sectors. If we cannot match to either the annual BR files or the LBD, we assign a NAICS sector based on the job type code found on the W-2 record. The main job type of concern to our analysis does not match to the BR and LBD is local government and we create a new NAICS sector called "other government" to handle these jobs.[7] However, there are a few W-2 reports that are coded as

---

[7]Self-employment jobs also do not match to either the BR or the LBD but these jobs are dropped from our analysis.

regular employment but still do not match and these jobs are consequently missing NAICS sector.

Of sons' jobs that match to the LBD or BR, 52.2% of them are with single-unit firms. These companies have a single industry classification and generally operate in only one location. For these types of employers, assigning the child an industry code is straight forward. However, the remaining jobs are with multi-unit firms, meaning the firm operates separate units in multiple locations, and these units may or may not be in the same NAICS sector. In our data, 29.8% of firms that employ sons are multi-units but only operate in one major NAICS sector while 16.6% are multi-units that operate in at least 2 different major NAICS sectors.[8] For these jobs, it is unclear how to assign an industry code to the worker since the W-2 gives only the parent company identifier and not the actual establishment identifier. To handle this problem caused by insufficient data, we create a weight for each NAICS sector found within a company. The weight for a given sector is equal to the percentage of total company employment working at establishments in that sector. Weights sum to one across all the NAICS sectors present in a given company.

There are EINs in the LBD and DER that do not have a NAICS sector and there are other EINs that have a NAICS sector but have missing employment totals. When a NAICS code is identified for a single-unit firm, it is kept regardless of the presence of employment totals because we do not need employment weights to assign multiple industry sectors. However when we encounter missing employment totals at multi-units, we only assign a NAICS sector if there is only one sector reported. For all cases where NAICS is missing, either due to insufficient information on the BR and LBD or because the EIN was not found in the LBD and BR, we create a "missing" sector and treat this as another industry sector in our summary statistics and regressions. Only 1.5% of sons' jobs are missing NAICS sector for any reason. Missing employment totals are more common with 7.3% missing for sons' jobs.

Our data has some advantages and disadvantages compared to the Swedish, Danish, and Canadian data used. Our major advantage compared to the Canadian and Danish data used by Bingley, Corak, and Westergard-Nielsen is that our family relationship between father and child is established by the survey whereas theirs is established by the tax data. Thus they are only able to look at fathers and sons who both worked and filed tax returns together when the son was a teenager. This clearly excludes sons who first worked at an older age and sons who filed independent tax returns once they were employed. This feature of the data may help explain the extremely high rate of shared employment when the fathers were very high earners. Teenagers of high earning fathers may be less likely to work overall and those who do may be disproportionately likely to work for their fathers.

Our main disadvantage relative to all three other data sources is our lack of knowledge about any child outcomes beyond formal employment and earnings. Because the SIPP panel is relatively short (maximum of four years), our only

---

[8]The remaining 1.4% of firms have missing firm structure information.

method of following the children into adulthood is to rely on the DER earnings history and the W-2 universe file. Thus we do not know how much education a child obtains, whether and at what age he or she marries, or what occupation he or she chooses. Thus it is difficult for us to control for all the important characteristics of a child that influence future outcomes. To mitigate the impact of these unobserved variables, we include child-fixed effects in our regressions whenever possible.

Finally while we have the universe of W-2 workers and firms in the year 2010, we do not have the same level of geographic knowledge about where the worker is located as is available in the Swedish data. In the U.S., multi-unit companies may choose to and commonly do file W-2 tax reports for a group of employees working at multiple plants using one common firm identifier. This prevents us from determining which workers share the same geographic location within employer and may over-state the rate of shared employment for big companies with locations spread across the country. We use the residence data from the MAF to try to counteract this lack of information, showing results for fathers and sons overall and fathers and sons who do not live close to each other.

4 Analysis and Results

4.1 Fathers and sons sharing employers

4.1.1 W-2 Universe Analysis

Using the set of fathers and sons from the SIPP matched with the universe of W-2s, we are able to calculate the frequency with which fathers and sons share employers.[9] We consider all employers of each father and son and categorize each son based on whether he shared any employer with his father in 2010. For this analysis, therefore, shared employment is a characteristic of each son (either he shares an employer with his father in 2010 or he does not). Because we do not have a long panel of this universe data, we can only identify contemporaneous employment and this prevents us from restricting attention to employers where the father preceded the son. We find that 9.6% of these sons shared an employer with their father in 2010. See Table 4.

We find that the probability that a son shares an employer with his father depends on the son's age. Over 12% of the youngest sons, who are between 15 and 17 in 2010, share an employer with their father. See Table 4. This is similar to the finding in Bingley, Corak, and Westergard-Nielsen that 10% of Danes and 8% of Canadians share an employer with their father at age 16. In our sample, 10.9% of sons who are 18 or 19 in 2010 share an employer with their father. This is comparable to the finding in Kramarz and Skans that just under 8% of new graduates in Sweden in 2002 share an employer with their father. The percentage of sons sharing employers with their fathers is greater than average

---

[9]We have not yet been able to do this calculation for daughters due to data access issues but hope to replicate these results for girls soon.

for the youngest sons (age 15–17) and lower than average for the oldest sons (ages 27–29 and 30–45).

We also find that the probability that a son shares an employer with his father depends on the father's earnings. Using the universe of W-2s, we calculate each father's location in the earnings distribution of men his age. The percentage of sons sharing employers with their fathers is less than average for the sons of the lowest-earning fathers (first decile) and higher than average for the sons of the highest-earning fathers (tenth decile). This contrasts with Bingley, Corak, and Westergard-Nielsen's finding of a u-shaped pattern in Canadian data, with both the lowest-earning and the highest-earning fathers more likely than average to share an employer with their sons. Figure 2 presents these results and the 95% confidence interval.

As explained above, some component of the rate at which fathers and sons share employers can be explained by the characteristics of the labor market. In other words, even if fathers did nothing to influence their sons' employment (or, indeed, even if fathers and sons were completely anonymous), there would be some sharing simply because there is a finite number of possible employers. It is therefore difficult to interpret measures of the intergenerational transmission of employers without reference to a baseline tendency of fathers to share jobs with men who are like their sons.

We construct this benchmark using the universe of 2010 W-2 data and our assignment of W-2 workers to geographic residence locations. For each son in our first sample, we create a group of neighbors who are all the workers in the same age bracket, earnings decile within that age bracket, and geographic location. We then compare the employers of the neighbors to the employer of the son's father in order to determine what percentage of neighbors work for the father's employer.[10] We treat this percentage as the baseline probability of working with the father, conditional on age, earnings, and geography. We average these probabilities across sons to create a baseline probability for the full sample. We then calculate the percentage of sons working at the same employer as their father and compare this to the baseline probability. If fathers do not help or influence the job search/hiring process of their sons in any way, we would expect that the percentage of sons sharing an employer would be equal to the baseline probability.

We consider four different geographic restrictions for the definitions of these sons' neighbors. The least restrictive geographic designation we analyze is men living in the same county as the son. The typical son has 840 neighbors in his county who are in his age group and in his decile of the earnings distribution for that age group. See Table 5. The other geographic regions (ZIP code, census tract, and census block group) are more restrictive than county, so that sons tend to have fewer neighbors under these definitions of neighbor. For example,

---

[10] When either the neighbors or the father have multiple jobs, we check for any employer matching by comparing all possible jobs to each other. It is also sometimes the case that individuals have more than one address in the MAF in a given year. We allow individuals to be part of multiple geographic groups based on these separate addresses when defining neighbors.

the typical son has 71 neighbors in his ZIP code and 51 neighbors in his census block group.

We find that fathers' and sons' tendency to share employers cannot be explained by the characteristics of the labor market alone: the probability that a father and son share an employer is much greater than the father's propensity to share an employer with other men who are very similar to his son. For example, while there is a 9.6% probability that a son shares a job with his father, only 0.5% of similar men living in his county share an employer with his father. See Table 6. The four different geographic restrictions generate average propensities of fathers to work with men like their sons of between 0.5% and 1.2%. In all cases, this baseline estimate is significantly lower than the observed rate of fathers and sons sharing employers. For the subsequent analyses we will focus on the ZIP-code definition of neighbor because is provides the highest, and therefore most conservative, benchmark.

We perform this baseline calculation separately for each age category, and we find that, at all ages, the probability that a son shares an employer with his father is significantly higher than the baseline. See Table 7.

We also calculate the baseline conditional on fathers' earnings, finding that the probability that a son shares an employer with his father is significantly higher than the baseline across the earnings distribution.

We also perform an analysis restricted to sons who are geographically removed from their fathers, as these are the sons who are least likely to share an employer with their fathers by chance. See Table 8. The probability that fathers and sons share an employer when they live in different states is 2.7%, the benchmark probability is 0.4%, and a t-test rejects the null hypothesis that the observed probability is equal to the benchmark.

4.1.2 DER Job History Analysis

For the next steps in our analysis, we look at both sons and daughters matched to the Detailed Earnings Record (DER). Using the DER instead of the universe of W-2s allows us to improve our analysis in two ways. First, we can look at jobs over the child's entire work history, not just in 2010. Second, we are able to restrict our attention to shared employers where the father preceded the child, which we consider to be the most important case for understanding the intergenerational transmission of employers. The cost of using the DER is that we no longer have the universe of data, and so cannot perform benchmark analyses for this sample that are equivalent to the ones we calculated for 2010. Summary statistics describing the sons in this sample show that most sons begin working as teenagers and 22% shared an employer with their father (simultaneously) at some point by age 30. See Table 9. At their first jobs, 6% of sons work for their fathers' employers, and at the highest-earning job at age 30, 3% of sons work with their fathers. For daughters, 13% shared an employer at some time by age 30 with 3% sharing at their first job and 2% sharing the highest paying job at 30.

However in contrast to the W-2 universe analysis, the unit of observation for this section is a job. Hence where shared employment was previously a characteristic of the child, it is now a characteristic of each job. Because of this, we should expect this measurement of shared employment to be lower than previously found. Consider a child with two jobs in 2010, one shared with his or her father and one unshared. In the previous analysis, this child is categorized as sharing an employer with his or her father. When looking at jobs, however, one job is categorized as shared and the other is categorized as unshared, so that, necessarily, the incidence of sharing is lower for jobs than it is for individuals. We find that approximately 2% of all sons' jobs are shared with their father and about 1% of all daughters' jobs. See Table 10.

We see significant differences between shared and unshared jobs, again shown in Table 10. The average unshared job for sons in our sample paid $8,695 (2011 dollars) a year, lasted approximately 2 years, and began when the son was between age 22 and 23. In contrast, the average shared job began when the son was younger (between 19 and 20), lasted longer (almost 4 years on average), and paid more on average ($11,470) but not in the first year of the job. Results for daughters are similar with shared jobs having higher earnings, longer tenure, and younger starting ages. The employer characteristics are also different between shared and unshared employers. For all children, shared jobs are more likely to be with single-unit firms and with employers with fewer than ten employees. For sons (but not daughters), shared jobs are less likely at employers with more than 1000 employees. For sons and daughters, shared jobs are more likely with employers in particular sectors, such as agriculture, manufacturing, and construction.

We categorize jobs by the age of the child in the first year on the job, and find a pattern consistent with our W-2 universe analysis: jobs started at a younger age are much more likely to have a shared employer, and jobs started at the oldest ages are less likely than average to have a shared employer. See Tables 11A and 11B. We also categorize the jobs by the father's location in the average earnings distribution, with the average calculated over the years when the child was between 15 and 19 years old. Consistent again with our previous analysis, we find that the jobs of children of the lowest-earning fathers are less likely than average to have a shared employer, while the jobs of the children of the highest-earning fathers are more likely than average to share employers.

We next consider which characteristics of the child and the father are likely to predict shared employment by estimating probit models, controlling first for child age and father race and education level. See Tables 12A and 12B. Initially for sons, we find no significant correlation with education but find that jobs held by sons of black fathers are approximately 3% less likely to be shared and that the probability of sharing is lower for older sons. When we add controls for father's location in the average earnings distribution when the son was a teenager (see column (2)), we see that jobs held by sons of the lowest-earning fathers are the least likely to be shared. We also see significant correlation between employer characteristics and the probability of sharing a job. In our specification that includes only firm structure and size, we find that job sharing is less likely at multi-units and less likely at larger firms. While the multi-unit result becomes insignificant when we add industry sector controls, firm size remains negatively correlated with the likelihood that sons and fathers will work at the same firm. Rates of job sharing also appears to be different across major NAICS sectors. With the professional, scientific, and technical industry sector serving as the baseline, jobs are more likely to be shared in agriculture, mining, construction, utilities, manufacturing, wholesale trade, transportation and warehousing, education, health care and social services, and public administration and are less likely to be shared in retail, information, administrative support and waste management, arts and recreation, and accommodation and food services. For the remaining five industry sectors, there is no significant correlation with job sharing. These results are consistent with the job-level summary statistics and would seem to indicate that fathers and sons are more likely to share jobs in higher skill industries. Combined with the result that fathers in higher average earnings deciles are more likely to share jobs with sons, the data seem to point to father and sons sharing employers as a phenomenon of more well-off families where the father has a career job that requires skill.

The probit results for daughters (see Table 12B) have similar patterns. Older daughters are less likely to share jobs and daughters of higher earning fathers are more likely. Interestingly, the effect of father education is significant in all the daughter probit specifications for the college and graduate degree education levels. Job sharing seems to be more prevalent among daughters with well-educated fathers. Our data provide no clues as to why this might be true but one might speculate that more educated fathers have a higher expectation that their daughters will work and have careers and hence are more likely to invest in helping their daughters get started in the labor market. It is also possible that these fathers work in jobs that involve less manual labor and hence are more attractive to daughters. The pattern of correlation between father/daughter job sharing and industry sector is remarkably similar to that of the father/son pattern. Information, education, and health care and social assistance are no longer associated with statistically significant higher levels of job sharing, and the other government sector now is. All other industries have effects of the same sign and significance. Like sons, jobs held by daughters in sectors like manufacturing and construction are more likely to be shared jobs. Firm size patterns are also similar to those of sons. Jobs at multi-units and larger firms are less likely to be shared.

The results on firm characteristics raise the possibility that fathers help their children get jobs in industry sectors where they would otherwise not find employment. Connections with the father help the child enter a more skilled industry, perhaps earlier in his or her career than would otherwise be possible. However it is also possible that the industry patterns simply reflect the location of most fathers later in their own careers. Jobs are more likely to be shared in manufacturing or wholesale trade simply because this is where the fathers are most likely to work. More work is needed to distinguish between these hypotheses.

4.2 Shared employers and sons' earnings

Having demonstrated the extent of the intergenerational transmission of employers in the U.S., we now evaluate whether this phenomenon could plausibly explain some of the correlation between fathers' and children's earnings. Once the SIPP panels end, we do not know any future outcomes of the children except what is found in the DER. Hence we focus exclusively on earnings and the relationship between what a child is paid by an employer and whether that employer was shared. In all analyses, we include controls for age, experience, tenure, and calendar year. Where possible, we take advantage of the panel nature of our data and perform fixed effects analyses to remove the unobserved characteristics of sons that are constant over time.

We first examine simple summary statistics and show that both sons' and daughters' average log earnings at jobs with shared employers are higher than those with unshared employers. See Tables 11A and 11B. We find that sons' earnings at shared jobs are higher for jobs started at all ages. We also investigate sons' earnings from shared employers across the fathers' earnings distribution. For the sons of lowest-earning fathers (first and second decile), t-tests fail to reject the null hypothesis that earnings are equal between shared and unshared jobs. For the sons of all other fathers, however, average log earnings are significantly higher at shared jobs. For daughters of the highest-earning fathers (ninth and tenth deciles of the earnings distribution), shared jobs are associated with higher earnings. For daughters of the lowest-earning fathers (first and second deciles), we find no statistically significant difference in the earnings at shared and unshared jobs.

We next turn to earnings regressions. In our simplest specification, we regress sons' earnings from each employer on an indicator for whether he shared that employer with his father. See Table 13A. The results in column 1 indicate that sons' earnings at shared employers are higher than their earnings at unshared employers. Column two includes an indicator for an alternative definition of shared employer: one where the father preceded the son but left before the son started. The results of this analysis suggest that it is the simultaneity of the job that is associated with higher earnings. In other words, what matters is not working where your father has worked, but rather working where your father does work. The third column shows coefficients on the interactions of age category and the shared employment indicator in order to break down the overall effect of shared employment into age specific effects. We find that the relationship between earnings and shared employer is significant for all but the youngest sons (age 15–17). Unlike with sons, the correlation between daughters' shared employment, either simultaneous or not, and earnings is not statistically significant at a 95-percent confidence level. Only for jobs shared when the daughter is age 18-19 is there a statistically significant positive coefficient on job sharing.

In Table 14A we present the results of our analysis of whether the relationship between shared employers and sons' earnings depends on fathers' average earnings as measured when the son between age 15 and 19. Because this measure of fathers' earnings is time invariant, we are unable to use fixed effects estimation. In column 1 of Table 14A, we present the OLS analog to column 1 of Table 13A, including fathers' quartile in the earnings distribution. We find that fathers' earnings are strongly (and positively) correlated with sons' earnings. In column 2 of Table 14A we present analysis that interacts job sharing with fathers' location in the average earnings distribution. We find no correlation between earnings and shared employment for sons of the lowest-earning fathers (first quartile of the earnings distribution), but a positive correlation for all other fathers. This suggests that when high-earning fathers help their sons find a job with their own employer, they may provide a greater earnings advantage to their sons relative to what low-earning fathers are able to do. Results for daughters in Table 14B show that shared employment is only correlated with higher earnings if the father had average earnings in the top quartile.

In Tables 15 and 16 we expand the fixed effects earnings regressions to include the following employer characteristics: firm type as multi-unit or single-unit, firm employment size (8 categories), and major NAICS sector (22 categories). When we include only firm type and firm size as controls, we still find correlation between shared employer and earnings (column 1). Interacting firm size and shared employment indicates that higher earnings are associated with shared jobs at larger employers (firms with more than 200 employees). The inclusion of NAICS sector controls still finds a statistically significant correlation between shared employment and earnings. This result would seem to indicate that some of the earnings boost that appears to come from sharing a job with a father is in fact simply an artifact of the industry of that job. Shared jobs pay more precisely because they are in higher paying industries like manufacturing and once industry is controlled for, the effect is greatly diminished. When we interact job sharing and industry, we find that for most industries, father-son shared jobs are not associated with higher earnings compared to non-shared jobs in the same industry. There are some exceptions to this general finding. Using a 95-percent confidence level, we find significantly lower earnings at shared jobs in wholesale trade and arts, entertainment, and recreation sectors and significantly higher earnings in shared jobs in administrative support and waste management and accommodation and food services sectors. It is possible that in these lower-skilled industries, shared employment is more important than in more skilled industries and that the father helps the son get a better paid position than he would otherwise. In contrast, in skilled industries, the father's contribution is to get the son a job he would not otherwise have gotten but once at that job, the son is paid similarly to other workers in the industry. However we are cautious about interpreting these results too strongly. The magnitude of the significant coefficients on the industry-job sharing interaction terms is large enough that we question whether these are realistic effects. They may be due to small sample sizes or to large amounts of job heterogeneity within these five sectors. For example if shared jobs in the administrative support and waste management sector are all concentrated in certain higher-paying three digit NAICS sectors, then these may be very different kinds of jobs than unshared jobs and the higher pay would simply be the result of comparing dissimilar jobs.

Likewise our models are not sufficient to distinguish between whether sons are actually holding jobs in different industries than they otherwise would due to sharing employers with their fathers or whether job sharing just happens in these industries because that is where fathers are more likely to work. More work is needed to determine whether job sharing has a true causal effect.

For daughters, the correlation between job sharing and earnings is still not statistically significant. When we interact industry and job sharing, only one industry has a positive significant coefficient (administrative support and waste management) whereas three industries have significant negative interactions (information, professional, scientific, and technical services, and health care and social assistance). Again we caution against over-interpreting these coefficients as the source of earnings differences within industry may be the result of some unobserved job characteristic rather than the sharing of employers.

Finally in Table 17A we isolate our analyses to particular jobs held by the sons. In columns 1 and 2 we investigate the relationship between earnings at the son's first employer and his father's employment at the same firm. We find a strong relationship, indicating that sons' earnings at first jobs are higher when they share their employer with their father. This correlation persists when we include firm characteristics. In columns 3 and 4 we consider sons' highest-paying job at age 30. We find that a son's earnings tend to be higher when this employer is shared with his father. When firm characteristics are added, we find no statistically significant difference in earnings at shared jobs. For daughters (Table 17B), we see no significant effects of shared employment at either first jobs or the highest paying job at age 30, regardless of whether firm characteristics are included.

5 Conclusion

We find substantial evidence that family networks influence labor market outcomes for sons. Conditional on age, earnings decile, and residential location, fathers and sons work together at the same employer more commonly than would be predicted by mere chance. While there is an initial positive correlation between job sharing and sons' earnings, we show that most of this correlation can be explained by the industry of the shared job. Job sharing is more common in higher paying industries and compared to unshared jobs in the same industry, shared jobs do not generally pay more. These results lead to the question of whether the father's main contribution in helping his son find employment is procuring a job at a higher paying firm than the son would otherwise qualify for on his own. More work is needed to determine if sons' job characteristics are in fact influenced by job sharing.

For daughters the results are more clear. Job sharing seems to have limited effects on earnings and is less common than with sons, seeming to be more exclusively the characteristic of a well-off family. Here the interesting question remains, why do daughters share jobs with their fathers less often than sons and how does this influence women's career paths relative to men?

Our next steps will be to consider the role of employer characteristics in determining the baseline matching probability from our first stage of analysis. Fathers and sons sharing employers may, to some extent, be caused by sharing a profession. If sons are likely to follow their fathers' education paths, they may end up at the same employer simply by virtue of working in the same field and not because of their fathers' influence in procuring employment. In this case, the father is still influencing the employment of his son but in a different manner. While we do not have data on the son's occupation, we will use industry as a proxy for the type of work done at the employer and will examine the propensity for employer sharing within industry groups. We will again rely on matching neighbors with the same industry as the son to determine a baseline matching rate to compare to the son matching rate. This will enable us to tell whether sons are more likely than unrelated neighbors to work for the same employer as their fathers given that they are in the same industry. In other words, this provides an estimate of any extra tendency on the part of sons to work for their fathers' employers even after they have chosen the same field of work. We can also consider whether fathers are changing the industry distribution of sons by procuring them employment or whether sons have the same industry distribution as matching neighbors. This will shed light on whether fathers are helping sons earn more than they otherwise would by finding them jobs in higher paying industries.

In addition to further work with employer characteristics, we also plan to examine son heterogeneity more thoroughly by adding more childhood characteristics of sons to our data. In particular, we will consider whether sons who showed potential for high earnings by excelling in school as teenagers were more or less likely to share employers than sons who had trouble at school. These correlations will help shed light on the potential bias in our estimates resulting from fathers' choices about which sons to help.

Finally, another outcome of the son that may be impacted by employer sharing is attachment to the labor market. Perhaps fathers are able to help their sons find jobs when they would otherwise be unemployed, thus increasing total years of labor market experience. A son may also enter the formal labor market for the first time at a younger age if his father helps him find a job, again leading to more overall experience and better long term labor market outcomes. We will estimate the relationship between shared employment and labor force attachment in order to determine if this is another potential avenue for the transmission of economic advantage.

References

[1] Paul Bingley, Miles Corak, and Niels Westergard-Nielsen. Equality of opportunity and intergenerational transmission of employers. *From Parents to Children: The Intergenerational Transmission of Advantage*, pages 441–460, 2012.

[2] Sandra E Black and Paul J Devereux. Recent developments in intergenerational mobility. *Handbook of labor economics*, 4:1487–1541, 2011.

[3] Miles Corak and Patrizio Piraino. The intergenerational transmission of employers. *Journal of Labor Economics*, 29(1):37–68, 2011.

[4] Judith K Hellerstein and Melinda Sandler Morrill. Dads and daughters the changing impact of fathers on women's occupational choices. *Journal of Human Resources*, 46(2):333–372, 2011.

[5] Markus Jantti, Bernt Bratsberg, Knut Røed, Oddbjorn Raaum, Robin Naylor, Eva Osterbacka, Anders Bjorklund, and Tor Eriksson. American exceptionalism in a new light: a comparison of intergenerational earnings mobility in the nordic countries, the united kingdom and the united states. 2006.

[6] Francis Kramarz and Oskar Nordström Skans. With a little help from my... parents? family networks and youth labor market entry. 2010.

[7] Francisco Pérez-González. Inherited control and firm performance. *The American Economic Review*, pages 1559–1588, 2006.

Table 1
Sample of Sons and Fathers Matched to W-2s and Master Address File

	Sons		Fathers	
	Individuals	Jobs	Individuals	Jobs
Sample from SIPP	35,454		26,761	
Sons matched to 2010 W-2s	24,756	37,102	19,635	
Sons matched to MAF	23,774	35,785	19,006	
Fathers matched to 2010 W-2s	16,487	32,144	13,082	16,475

The initial sample from the SIPP includes sons who are no older than 17 at the time of the survey, who are at least 15 by 2010, who have a valid Social Security Number, who live with their father at the time of the survey, and whose father has a valid Social Security Number. SIPP respondents were taken from the 1984, 1990, 1991, 1992, 1993, 1996, 2001, 2004, and 2008 SIPP panels.

Table 2
Fathers that did not match to 2010 W-2s

	Percent
Does not link to any administrative data	0.1%
Amended W-2 filed later	0.3%
Self-employed	18.9%
Receiving OASDI benefits	41.7%
Deceased	6.0%
Unknown	33.1%

This breakdown describes the 5,924 fathers who did not match to an IRS Form W-2 from 2010.

Failure to link to any administrative data is likely the result of an incorrect or invalid SSN.

Some individuals filed amended W-2s late enough that they were not present in the universe of W-2 records but were present in the SSA DER file.

Fathers are categorized as self-employed if all earnings in 2010 were from self-employment.

OASDI beneficiaries include those receiving retirement, spousal, or disability benefits.

Fathers who failed to match for unknown reasons include the unemployed, those out of the labor force, those with informal employment, and emigrants.

Table 3

Panel A Sample of Sons age 30 or older by 2011

	Sons		Fathers	
	Individuals	Jobs	Individuals	Jobs
Sample from SIPP (1)	9,503		7,952	
Sons matched to DER (2)	9,416	126,049	7,896	
Fathers matched to DER (3)	9,353	125,243	7,849	98,611
Only jobs that are not self-employment (4)	9,339	121,896	7,840	

Panel B Sample of Daughters age 30 or older by 2011

	Daughters		Fathers	
	Individuals	Jobs	Individuals	Jobs
Sample from SIPP (1)	8,595		7,290	
Daughters matched to DER (2)	8,540	109,526	7,251	
Fathers matched to DER (3)	8,463	108,507	7,192	88,367
Only jobs that are not self-employment (4)	8,458	105,809	7,187	

The initial sample from the SIPP in row (1) includes sons/daughters who are no older than 17 at the time of the survey, who are at least 30 by 2010, who have a valid Social Security Number, who live with their father at the time of the survey, and whose father has a valid Social Security Number. Only SIPP respondents from the 1984, 1990, 1991, 1992, 1993, and 1996 panels were used. Respondents who were 17 and younger in the 2000s decade did not reach age 30 by 2010 and were excluded from our sample.

Row (2) drops sons/daughters who never match to the DER. Row (3) drops sons/daughters whose fathers never match to the DER. Row (4) drops self-employment jobs for sons/daughters, which also eliminates sons/daughters who never have regular employer jobs.

Table 4
Fathers and Sons Sharing Employers in 2010

	Number of sons	% at same employer	t-statistic
All	16,487	9.6%	N/A
Age categories			
15-17	861	12.5%	2.53
18-19	2,258	10.9%	1.88
20-21	2,532	10.8%	1.81
22-23	2,447	10.7%	1.56
24-26	2,860	9.1%	-0.99
27-29	2,316	8.2%	-2.32
30-45	3,213	7.7%	-3.59
Father's earnings decile			
1st	1,210	7.4%	-2.90
2nd	1,323	8.4%	-1.56
3rd	1,475	9.4%	-0.35
4th	1,587	10.6%	1.18
5th	1,675	8.7%	-1.35
6th	1,789	9.3%	-0.41
7th	1,893	9.3%	-0.47
8th	1,814	10.0%	0.47
9th	1,859	9.8%	0.29
10th	1,809	12.5%	3.59

Employers are defined by the IRS-assigned Employer Identification Number (EIN). Fathers and sons are considered to share an employer in 2010 if they both had a Form W-2 filed by the same employer for calendar year 2010.

Ages categories are based on the age of the son on December 31, 2010. The father's earnings decile is calculated as his location in the 2010 earnings distribution of all men his age.

t-statistics from tests of equality between the categories and the overall sample mean.

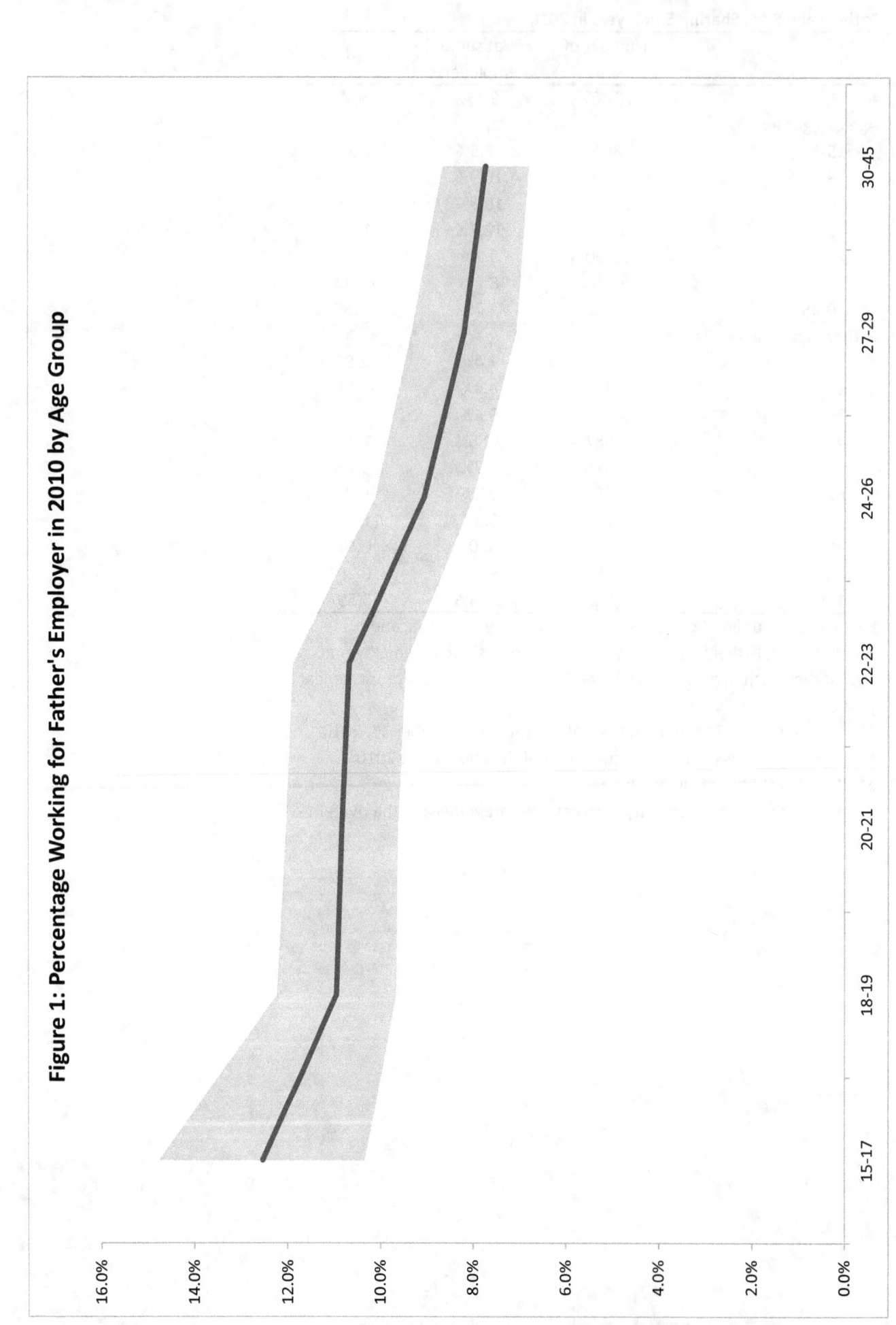

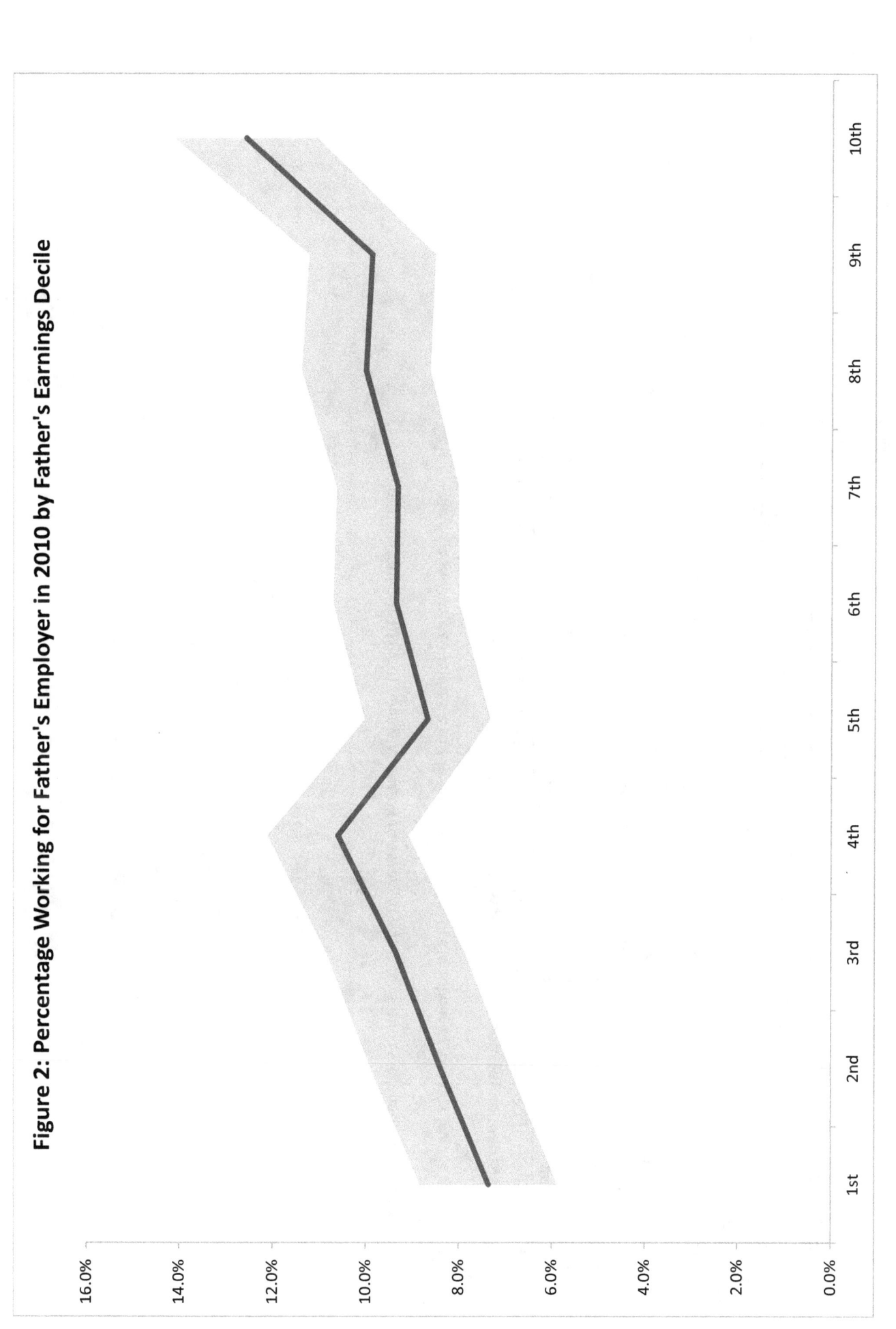

Table 5
Distributions of Number of Neighbors

	Same county	Same ZIP code	Same Census tract	Same Census block group
Mean	3,142.95	155.62	1,020.55	350.91
Percentiles				
5th percentile	37	6	8	3
10th percentile	74	11	13	4
25th percentile	247	30	41	12
50th percentile	840	71	197	51
75th percentile	2,512	166	931	215
90th percentile	7,402	377	2,484	617
95th percentile	13,056	584	4,521	1,143

For each son, the set of neighbors is defined as the men who are in his age category, who are in his decile of the earnings distribution for men that age, and who are in his geographic area (e.g., in the same county).

For example, the typical son has 71 neighbors in his zip code who are of a similar age and who have similar earnings.

The set of all possible neighbors comes from the universe of Forms W-2 filed in 2010 and matched to the MAF.

Table 6
Counterfactual Fathers and Sons Sharing Employers

	% at same employer
Sons	9.6%
Neighbors	
Same county	0.5%
	(39.38)
Same ZIP code	1.2%
	(35.91)
Same Census tract	0.5%
	(39.66)
Same Census block group	1.0%
	(36.60)

The row labeled "Sons" reports the number of sons in the sample who share an employer with their father in 2010.

For each son, the percentage of his neighbors within a certain geographic area that work for the same employer as his father is calculated. The average of this percentage across all sons is reported in subsequent rows, labeled by type of geographic area. A t-statistic is reported for a test of equality between the percentage of sons who share an employer with their fathers and the average percentage of neighbors who share an employer with the sons' fathers.

Table 7
Neighbors in the Same ZIP Code

	Sons	Neighbors	t-statistic
All	9.6%	1.2%	35.91
Age categories			
15-17	12.5%	3.3%	7.66
18-19	10.9%	1.6%	13.89
20-21	10.8%	1.5%	14.70
22-23	10.7%	1.1%	15.15
24-25	9.1%	0.9%	14.94
26-30	8.2%	1.0%	12.46
31-45	7.7%	0.7%	14.93
Father's earnings decile			
1st	7.4%	1.2%	8.01
2nd	8.4%	1.2%	9.18
3rd	9.4%	1.3%	10.45
4th	10.6%	1.4%	11.55
5th	8.7%	1.2%	10.70
6th	9.3%	1.2%	11.63
7th	9.3%	1.1%	12.09
8th	10.0%	1.3%	12.04
9th	9.8%	1.3%	12.14
10th	12.5%	1.1%	14.62

A comparison of results for sons (see Table 4) with sons' neighbors. t-statistics in each row from a test of equality between the sons and the neighbors benchmark.

Table 8
Shared employers for sons living away from fathers

Sample	Number	% at same employer	% of neighbors at same	t-statistic
All sons	16,487	9.6%	1.2%	35.91
In different ZIP code than father	5,977	5.1%	0.7%	15.28
In different state than father	2,488	2.7%	0.4%	6.97

An analysis restricted to sons living away from their fathers. t-statistics in each row from a test of equality between the sons and the neighbors benchmark.

Table 9
Descriptive Statistics: Children and Fathers

	Sons	Daughters
Child characteristics		
Black	0.08	0.08
	(0.27)	(0.27)
Number of jobs	13.05	12.51
	(8.66)	(7.43)
Age in 2010	32.58	32.59
	(3.24)	(3.25)
Age at first job	16.51	16.64
	(1.79)	(1.71)
Worked between ages of 12 and 19	0.96	0.96
	(0.19)	(0.20)
First year earnings at first job	$2,126.77	$1,925.89
	(2518.90)	(2120.38)
First job was self-employment	0.01	0.01
	(0.11)	(0.09)
Earnings from the highest-paying job at age 30	$41,344.40	$31,274.17
	(50625.36)	(25868.47)
Ever had the same employer as father	0.28	0.17
	(0.45)	(0.38)
Ever had the same employer as father (simultaneous)	0.22	0.13
	(0.41)	(0.33)
Father worked at son's first employer	0.06	0.03
	(0.23)	(0.17)
Father worked at son's highest-earning job at age 30	0.03	0.02
	(0.18)	(0.12)
Father Characteristics		
Black	0.08	0.08
	(0.27)	(0.27)
Age in 2010	61.06	61.09
	(7.11)	(7.26)
Less than high school education	0.16	0.16
	(0.37)	(0.37)
High school diploma	0.32	0.31
	(0.47)	(0.46)
Some College	0.24	0.25
	(0.43)	(0.43)
College diploma	0.15	0.14
	(0.36)	(0.35)
Graduate education	0.10	0.10
	(0.30)	(0.30)
Average annual earnings when son aged 15-19	$64,632.64	$65,023.32
	(90442.88)	(76172.43)
N	9,339	8,458

These samples of sons and daughters are described in Panel A row (4) and Panel B row (4) respectively of Table 3. Standard deviations in parentheses.

Table 10
Descriptive Statistics: Children's Jobs

	Sons			Daughters		
	Shared	Unshared	t-statistic	Shared	Unshared	t-statistic
Number of years at job	3.91	2.05	23.15	3.58	2.10	14.50
Age child began job	19.94	22.90	-34.29	19.96	22.74	-22.68
Age child left job	23.44	24.08	-5.50	23.11	23.95	-5.21
Average annual earnings	$11,470	$8,695	7.71	$7,782	$6,908	2.57
Earnings in first year	$6,320	$6,526	-1.04	$4,690	$5,168	-2.21
MU firm (EIN)	38.50%	45.47%	-6.93	41.42%	48.47%	-4.79
Firm Size						
Under 10	15.55%	9.67%	7.88	16.09%	9.08%	6.41
10-25	12.50%	10.13%	3.48	10.03%	9.73%	0.33
26-50	9.62%	8.30%	2.16	8.27%	7.65%	0.75
51-100	7.86%	8.01%	-0.26	5.98%	7.29%	-1.85
101-200	7.78%	7.07%	1.27	5.28%	6.81%	-2.30
201-500	8.40%	8.60%	-0.34	8.71%	8.46%	0.30
501-1000	6.23%	6.04%	0.38	6.60%	6.27%	0.44
1000+	28.18%	32.61%	-4.76	34.92%	35.64%	-0.51
Missing	3.89%	9.58%	-14.07	4.13%	9.07%	-8.26
Employer sector						
Agriculture, Forestry, Fishing	3.24%	1.13%	5.90	2.78%	0.51%	4.74
Mining	1.06%	0.41%	3.24	0.57%	0.06%	2.43
Utilities	0.49%	0.14%	2.53	0.74%	0.08%	2.68
Construction	13.91%	7.65%	8.83	5.36%	0.96%	6.59
Manufacturing	18.10%	7.01%	14.50	15.74%	3.40%	11.80
Wholesale	6.92%	3.16%	7.64	5.90%	1.72%	6.31
Retail	10.12%	15.11%	-8.18	11.03%	17.86%	-7.45
Transportation & Warehousing	3.32%	2.53%	2.17	2.03%	0.85%	2.91
Information	1.07%	1.94%	-4.20	2.05%	1.86%	0.46
Finance & Insurance	1.91%	2.05%	-0.51	2.21%	3.64%	-3.27
Real Estate and Rental	1.35%	1.50%	-0.66	1.23%	1.40%	-0.53
Professional, Scientific, Technical	3.57%	3.70%	-0.37	5.37%	4.47%	1.37
Management	0.24%	0.71%	-9.08	0.25%	0.78%	-5.31
Administrative	5.84%	13.62%	-16.08	4.64%	10.76%	-9.78
Education	5.66%	3.00%	5.60	8.59%	5.68%	3.50
Health Care	5.78%	3.56%	4.67	8.65%	11.72%	-3.69
Arts	1.22%	2.30%	-4.86	1.65%	2.22%	-1.52
Accomodation & Food	3.17%	14.67%	-31.28	6.08%	17.04%	-15.31
Other	3.60%	3.34%	0.70	4.60%	3.79%	1.30
Public	3.69%	1.48%	5.71	3.87%	1.36%	4.38
Other Government	1.92%	1.41%	1.83	2.73%	0.80%	3.99
Missing industry sector	1.63%	3.73%	-7.93	1.93%	3.68%	-4.23
Foreign	0.00%	0.02%	-3.43	0.00%	0.01%	-5.12
N	2,392	119,504		1,137	104,672	

This sample of jobs is described in Panel A row (4) of Table 3 and does not include self-employment. t-statistics are for tests of equality between shared and unshared jobs.

Table 11A
Sons' Earnings in Shared and Unshared Jobs

	Number	% shared	t-statistic	Average log earnings		
				Unshared	Shared	t-statistic
All jobs	120,856	2.0%	N/A	7.77	8.37	18.38
Age categories						
12-17	15,045	4.4%	14.28	6.93	7.75	13.73
18-19	22,058	3.1%	8.85	7.25	8.35	19.78
20-21	20,012	2.0%	-0.05	7.50	8.45	11.90
22-23	16,651	1.4%	-6.07	7.85	8.81	9.50
24-25	19,009	1.1%	-10.14	8.16	9.13	8.91
26-30	13,513	0.9%	-11.46	8.39	9.01	4.11
31-45	14,568	0.6%	-18.61	8.55	9.10	3.01
Father's earnings decile						
1st	10,084	0.4%	-21.56	7.52	7.54	0.07
2nd	11,803	1.4%	-5.44	7.61	7.71	0.83
3rd	12,848	2.0%	0.44	7.67	8.06	4.13
4th	12,352	2.2%	1.76	7.66	8.25	6.42
5th	12,861	2.4%	2.73	7.78	8.35	6.71
6th	12,785	2.2%	1.92	7.81	8.33	5.82
7th	12,041	2.0%	0.20	7.81	8.53	6.31
8th	12,891	2.0%	0.50	7.86	8.48	5.95
9th	12,031	2.2%	1.86	7.91	8.67	8.01
10th	11,160	2.6%	4.01	8.02	8.79	8.07

Table 11B
Daughters' Earnings in Shared and Unshared Jobs

	Number	% shared	t-statistic	Average log earnings		
				Unshared	Shared	t-statistic
All jobs	105,018	1.1%	N/A	7.63	7.98	7.38
Age categories						
12-17	13,163	2.3%	9.34	6.90	7.44	7.02
18-19	19,361	1.6%	5.31	7.15	7.83	7.84
20-21	18,072	1.2%	0.83	7.36	8.02	5.66
22-23	14,876	0.8%	-3.32	7.78	8.40	4.02
24-25	16,377	0.6%	-6.60	8.07	8.81	4.89
26-30	11,405	0.4%	-9.83	8.23	8.51	1.05
31-45	11,764	0.3%	-11.85	8.23	9.05	4.38
Father's earnings decile						
1st	8,940	0.2%	-15.37	7.43	7.06	-1.21
2nd	9,845	0.8%	-2.91	7.48	7.53	0.37
3rd	10,795	0.9%	-1.99	7.51	7.86	2.36
4th	10,045	1.1%	-0.14	7.53	7.79	1.66
5th	10,722	1.2%	0.79	7.63	7.56	-0.52
6th	11,045	1.0%	-0.38	7.63	8.13	3.45
7th	10,558	1.1%	-0.18	7.68	8.11	2.89
8th	10,635	1.2%	1.12	7.75	7.97	1.48
9th	11,226	1.4%	2.90	7.80	8.22	3.06
10th	11,207	1.7%	5.18	7.79	8.32	4.91

Table 12A
Probability of Fathers and Sons Sharing Employers

	(1) Probit	(1) Marginal effects	(2) Probit	(2) Marginal effects	(3) Probit	(3) Marginal effects	(4) Probit	(4) Marginal effects
Father black	-0.29	-0.03	-0.25	-0.01	-0.23	-0.01	-0.20	-0.01
	(-7.56)	(-6.98)	(-6.32)	(-4.72)	(-5.85)	(-4.57)	(-4.82)	(-3.73)
Father education								
High school	0.01	0.00	-0.06	0.00	-0.06	0.00	-0.05	0.00
	(0.58)	(0.58)	(-2.17)	(-2.11)	(-2.16)	(-2.10)	(-1.78)	(-1.72)
Some college	0.00	0.00	-0.09	0.00	-0.09	0.00	-0.05	0.00
	(0.06)	(0.06)	(-3.31)	(-3.12)	(-3.31)	(-3.12)	(-1.74)	(-1.69)
College	-0.03	0.00	-0.15	0.00	-0.15	-0.01	-0.10	-0.01
	(-1.07)	(-1.07)	(-4.50)	(-4.12)	(-4.58)	(-4.16)	(-2.92)	(-2.73)
Graduate	0.05	0.01	-0.08	0.00	-0.09	0.00	-0.03	0.00
	(1.58)	(1.56)	(-2.27)	(-2.30)	(-2.37)	(-2.39)	(-0.86)	(-0.87)
Age categories								
18-19	-0.17	-0.01	-0.17	0.00	-0.17	-0.01	-0.30	-0.01
	(-6.82)	(-6.50)	(-6.79)	(-5.02)	(-6.74)	(-5.05)	(-11.03)	(-5.22)
20-21	-0.35	-0.02	-0.35	-0.01	-0.35	-0.01	-0.52	-0.02
	(-12.98)	(-11.58)	(-12.82)	(-6.42)	(-12.76)	(-6.45)	(-17.32)	(-5.47)
22-23	-0.50	-0.03	-0.49	-0.01	-0.50	-0.01	-0.68	-0.02
	(-15.88)	(-14.00)	(-15.69)	(-6.67)	(-15.72)	(-6.69)	(-19.80)	(-5.45)
24-26	-0.58	-0.03	-0.58	-0.01	-0.58	-0.02	-0.78	-0.02
	(-18.29)	(-15.24)	(-18.14)	(-6.74)	(-18.12)	(-6.75)	(-22.43)	(-5.43)
27-29	-0.65	-0.04	-0.64	-0.01	-0.65	-0.02	-0.86	-0.02
	(-17.18)	(-15.61)	(-16.99)	(-6.73)	(-17.02)	(-6.73)	(-21.07)	(-5.41)
30-45	-0.81	-0.04	-0.81	-0.01	-0.81	-0.02	-1.03	-0.02
	(-19.25)	(-16.90)	(-19.15)	(-6.75)	(-19.11)	(-6.74)	(-22.98)	(-5.38)
Father's earn. decile								
2nd			0.44	0.02	0.45	0.03	0.45	0.04
			(7.01)	(7.28)	(7.04)	(7.14)	(6.85)	(6.05)
3rd			0.62	0.04	0.62	0.05	0.65	0.07
			(10.23)	(10.71)	(10.17)	(10.19)	(10.20)	(8.07)
4th			0.65	0.04	0.65	0.06	0.67	0.07
			(10.68)	(10.89)	(10.64)	(10.37)	(10.53)	(8.13)
5th			0.67	0.05	0.68	0.06	0.68	0.07
			(11.15)	(11.36)	(11.12)	(10.82)	(10.83)	(8.32)
6th			0.66	0.04	0.66	0.06	0.68	0.07
			(10.77)	(10.79)	(10.77)	(10.33)	(10.63)	(8.12)
7th			0.61	0.04	0.61	0.05	0.63	0.06
			(9.90)	(9.77)	(9.87)	(9.41)	(9.82)	(7.62)
8th			0.63	0.04	0.63	0.06	0.64	0.07
			(10.17)	(9.99)	(10.22)	(9.67)	(9.95)	(7.70)
9th			0.67	0.05	0.68	0.06	0.68	0.07
			(10.85)	(10.42)	(10.86)	(10.06)	(10.55)	(7.97)
10th			0.75	0.06	0.75	0.08	0.76	0.09
			(11.86)	(10.82)	(11.92)	(10.52)	(11.59)	(8.44)
Constant	-1.69		-2.23		-2.07		-1.99	
	(-66.85)		(-38.45)		(-33.27)		(-24.93)	
N	121,670		121,670		121,670		121,670	
Incl. firm size/struct.	no	no	no	no	yes	yes	yes	yes
Incl. firm industry	no	no	no	no	no	no	yes	yes

Results from a probit estimation of the probability of the son's job being at the same employer as the father. An observation is a job held by the son. This sample of jobs is described in Panel A row (4) of Table 3 and does not include self-employment. In addition, jobs at companies classified as "Foreign Sector" in the Census Business Register are dropped (201 jobs). Father's earnings decile calculated as father's place in the average earnings distribution with the average calculated in the five years when the son was age 15-19. Z-statistics in parentheses. Marginal effects calculated relative to a son age 15-17 holding a job in the Scientific, Professional, and Technical NAICS sector, at a single-unit firm with 1-9 employees and having a non-black father with less than a high school education in the first earnings decile.

Table 12A (cont.) Prob. of Fathers and Sons Sharing Employers

	(3)		(4)	
	Probit	Marginal effects	Probit	Marginal effects
Firm type=MU	-0.13	-0.01	0.03	0.00
	(-5.92)	(-4.69)	(1.14)	(1.12)
Firm size				
10-25 empl.	-0.11	0.00	-0.07	0.00
	(-3.20)	(-2.98)	(-1.85)	(-1.78)
26-50 empl.	-0.12	-0.01	-0.06	0.00
	(-3.30)	(-3.09)	(-1.63)	(-1.59)
51-100 empl.	-0.15	-0.01	-0.12	-0.01
	(-3.89)	(-3.59)	(-2.89)	(-2.70)
101-200 empl.	-0.08	0.00	-0.11	-0.01
	(-1.87)	(-1.87)	(-2.66)	(-2.53)
201-500 empl.	-0.09	0.00	-0.16	-0.01
	(-2.31)	(-2.28)	(-3.76)	(-3.34)
501-1000 empl.	-0.03	0.00	-0.11	-0.01
	(-0.79)	(-0.79)	(-2.31)	(-2.27)
1000+ empl.	-0.10	0.00	-0.13	-0.01
	(-3.01)	(-2.84)	(-3.47)	(-3.10)
firm size missing	-0.50	0.00	-0.50	-0.02
	(-10.36)	(0.00)	(-8.59)	(-5.18)
Industry Sector (2 digit NAICS)				
Agriculture			0.22	0.01
			(3.11)	(3.48)
Mining			0.49	0.03
			(4.40)	(4.11)
Utilities			0.64	0.04
			(4.15)	(3.76)
Construction			0.24	0.01
			(4.53)	(5.24)
Manufacturing			0.42	0.02
			(7.91)	(6.98)
Wholesale Trade			0.31	0.02
			(5.10)	(5.32)
Retail Trade			-0.36	-0.02
			(-6.55)	(-3.68)
Transp. & Wareh.			0.18	0.01
			(2.71)	(2.96)
Information			-0.30	-0.02
			(-3.19)	(-2.57)
Finance & Insurance			0.04	0.00
			(0.48)	(0.49)
Real Est. & Rental			-0.14	-0.01
			(-1.59)	(-1.44)
Mgt. of Companies			-0.40	-0.02
			(-1.68)	(-1.59)
Adm. Sup., Waste Mgt.			-0.28	-0.02
			(-4.93)	(-3.21)
Education			0.22	0.01
			(3.53)	(3.80)
Health C. & Social Asst.			0.19	0.01
			(3.21)	(3.59)
Arts, Entertm., Rec.			-0.47	-0.03
			(-5.50)	(-3.59)
Accomd. & Food			-0.79	-0.04
			(-12.68)	(-4.82)
Other Services			-0.11	-0.01
			(-1.72)	(-1.50)
Public Admin			0.33	0.02
			(4.62)	(4.67)
Other Government			0.13	0.01
			(1.57)	(1.65)
Missing			0.08	0.00
			(0.77)	(0.79)
	Probit	Marginal effects	Probit	Marginal effects

Table 12B
Probability of Fathers and Daughters Sharing Employers

	(1) Probit	(1) Marginal effects	(2) Probit	(2) Marginal effects	(3) Probit	(3) Marginal effects	(4) Probit	(4) Marginal effects
Father black	-0.16 (-3.30)	-0.01 (-3.11)	-0.13 (-2.62)	0.00 (-2.23)	-0.12 (-2.43)	0.00 (-2.14)	-0.09 (-1.78)	0.00 (-1.60)
Father education								
High school	0.06 (1.51)	0.00 (1.53)	0.00 (0.06)	0.00 (0.06)	0.00 (-0.07)	0.00 (-0.07)	0.04 (0.91)	0.00 (0.89)
Some college	0.12 (3.10)	0.01 (3.15)	0.05 (1.21)	0.00 (1.16)	0.04 (0.99)	0.00 (0.97)	0.10 (2.27)	0.00 (2.00)
College	0.26 (6.30)	0.01 (5.97)	0.16 (3.63)	0.00 (2.81)	0.15 (3.28)	0.00 (2.66)	0.21 (4.48)	0.01 (3.04)
Graduate	0.37 (8.67)	0.02 (7.59)	0.26 (5.44)	0.01 (3.48)	0.24 (4.95)	0.01 (3.40)	0.30 (5.95)	0.01 (3.43)
Age categories								
18-19	-0.16 (-4.75)	-0.01 (-4.43)	-0.16 (-4.77)	0.00 (-3.34)	-0.16 (-4.88)	0.00 (-3.44)	-0.23 (-6.38)	0.00 (-3.34)
20-21	-0.29 (-8.07)	-0.01 (-6.93)	-0.29 (-8.08)	0.00 (-4.03)	-0.30 (-8.27)	-0.01 (-4.14)	-0.39 (-9.92)	-0.01 (-3.59)
22-23	-0.43 (-10.48)	-0.01 (-8.57)	-0.43 (-10.44)	0.00 (-4.23)	-0.45 (-10.67)	-0.01 (-4.33)	-0.55 (-12.12)	-0.01 (-3.63)
24-26	-0.51 (-12.09)	-0.01 (-9.25)	-0.52 (-12.07)	0.00 (-4.27)	-0.53 (-12.34)	-0.01 (-4.37)	-0.65 (-13.85)	-0.01 (-3.63)
27-29	-0.65 (-11.84)	-0.01 (-9.80)	-0.65 (-11.78)	0.00 (-4.28)	-0.68 (-12.05)	-0.01 (-4.37)	-0.80 (-13.37)	-0.01 (-3.61)
30-45	-0.71 (-12.25)	-0.02 (-10.01)	-0.71 (-12.18)	0.00 (-4.28)	-0.74 (-12.47)	-0.01 (-4.37)	-0.86 (-13.84)	-0.01 (-3.61)
Father's earn. decile								
2nd			0.47 (5.35)	0.01 (5.37)	0.46 (5.31)	0.02 (5.20)	0.48 (5.26)	0.02 (4.47)
3rd			0.48 (5.63)	0.01 (5.74)	0.48 (5.58)	0.02 (5.52)	0.51 (5.60)	0.02 (4.72)
4th			0.54 (6.37)	0.02 (6.28)	0.54 (6.33)	0.03 (6.05)	0.58 (6.49)	0.03 (5.13)
5th			0.58 (6.82)	0.02 (6.66)	0.57 (6.80)	0.03 (6.39)	0.59 (6.66)	0.03 (5.24)
6th			0.52 (6.14)	0.02 (6.05)	0.52 (6.12)	0.02 (5.84)	0.54 (6.03)	0.03 (4.87)
7th			0.52 (6.14)	0.02 (5.95)	0.52 (6.10)	0.02 (5.74)	0.54 (6.00)	0.03 (4.82)
8th			0.56 (6.56)	0.02 (6.30)	0.56 (6.57)	0.03 (6.09)	0.57 (6.38)	0.03 (5.01)
9th			0.58 (6.91)	0.02 (6.56)	0.58 (6.91)	0.03 (6.33)	0.59 (6.63)	0.03 (5.12)
10th			0.62 (7.39)	0.02 (6.85)	0.63 (7.47)	0.03 (6.67)	0.66 (7.40)	0.04 (5.49)
Constant	-2.11 (-56.80)		-2.57 (-31.52)		-2.36 (-27.34)		-2.34 (-22.35)	
N	105,642		105,642		105,642		105,642	
Incl. firm size/struct.	no	no	no	no	yes	yes	yes	yes
Incl. firm industry	no	no	no	no	no	no	yes	yes

Results from a probit estimation of the probability of the daughter's job being at the same employer as the father. An observation is a job held by the daughter. This sample of jobs is described in Panel B row (4) of Table 3 and does not include self-employment. In addition, jobs at companies classified as "Foreign Sector" in the Census Business Register are dropped (201 jobs). Father's earnings decile calculated as father's place in the average earnings distribution with the average calculated in the five years when the daughter was age 15-19. Z-statistics in parentheses. Marginal effects calculated relative to a daughter age 15-17 holding a job in the Scientific, Professional, and Technical NAICS sector, at a single-unit firm with 1-9 employees and having a non-black father with less than a high school education in the first earnings decile.

Table 12B (cont.) Prob. of Fathers and Daughters Sharing Employers

	(3)		(4)	
	Probit	Marginal effects	Probit	Marginal effects
Firm type=MU	-0.17	0.00	0.02	0.00
	(-5.83)	(-3.71)	(0.46)	(0.45)
Firm size				
10-25 empl.	-0.20	0.00	-0.17	0.00
	(-4.24)	(-3.25)	(-3.31)	(-2.62)
26-50 empl.	-0.17	0.00	-0.15	0.00
	(-3.40)	(-2.88)	(-2.75)	(-2.36)
51-100 empl.	-0.23	0.00	-0.23	0.00
	(-4.09)	(-3.29)	(-3.92)	(-2.94)
101-200 empl.	-0.20	0.00	-0.28	-0.01
	(-3.47)	(-3.02)	(-4.33)	(-3.11)
201-500 empl.	-0.08	0.00	-0.18	0.00
	(-1.46)	(-1.45)	(-3.19)	(-2.62)
501-1000 empl.	-0.05	0.00	-0.17	0.00
	(-0.81)	(-0.82)	(-2.65)	(-2.37)
1000+ empl.	-0.05	0.00	-0.14	0.00
	(-1.22)	(-1.19)	(-2.76)	(-2.36)
firm size missing	-0.48	-0.01	-0.53	-0.01
	(-7.38)	(-4.15)	(-6.41)	(-3.52)
Industry Sector (2 digit NAICS)				
Agriculture			0.63	0.02
			(6.41)	(4.14)
Mining			1.07	0.03
			(4.46)	(3.19)
Utilities			1.11	0.03
			(5.71)	(3.54)
Construction			0.68	0.02
			(8.08)	(4.24)
Manufacturing			0.66	0.02
			(10.03)	(4.46)
Wholesale Trade			0.48	0.01
			(6.02)	(4.08)
Retail Trade			-0.35	-0.01
			(-5.45)	(-2.76)
Transp. & Wareh.			0.45	0.01
			(4.10)	(3.31)
Information			-0.05	0.00
			(-0.54)	(-0.52)
Finance & Insurance			-0.18	0.00
			(-1.91)	(-1.57)
Real Est. & Rental			-0.16	0.00
			(-1.39)	(-1.23)
Mgt. of Companies			-0.48	-0.01
			(-1.51)	(-1.39)
Adm. Sup., Waste Mgt.			-0.28	-0.01
			(-3.78)	(-2.39)
Education			0.11	0.00
			(1.52)	(1.61)
Health C. & Social Asst.			-0.10	0.00
			(-1.49)	(-1.25)
Arts, Entertm., Rec.			-0.26	-0.01
			(-2.59)	(-1.96)
Accomd. & Food			-0.55	-0.01
			(-8.00)	(-3.16)
Other Services			-0.02	0.00
			(-0.31)	(-0.30)
Public Admin			0.37	0.01
			(4.09)	(3.42)
Other Government			0.50	0.01
			(4.94)	(3.60)
Missing			0.13	0.00
			(0.96)	(0.98)

Table 13A
Fixed Effects Regressions of Sons' Earnings on Shared Employers

	(1)	(2)	(3)
Shared employer with father	0.22	0.22	
	(6.50)	(6.50)	
Shared employer with father (Non-simultaneous)		0.01	
		(0.25)	
Shared employer with father by age category			
12-17			0.06
			(1.11)
18-19			0.34
			(7.42)
20-21			0.26
			(5.16)
22-23			0.20
			(3.66)
24-25			0.15
			(2.50)
26-30			0.23
			(3.42)
31-45			0.23
			(2.98)
Observations (job-years)	252,809	252,809	252,853
Groups (persons)	9,337	9,337	9,337

Dependent variable is the natural log of the sons' earnings. All regressions include dummy variables for calendar year and son's age as well as measures of job tenure and total experience. t-statistics (in parentheses) are calculated with heteroskedasticity-robust standard errors.

Table 13B
Fixed Effects Regressions of Daughters' Earnings on Shared Employers

	(1)	(2)	(3)
Shared employer with father	0.08	0.08	
	(1.64)	(1.66)	
Shared employer with father (Non-simultaneous)		0.06	
		(0.76)	
Shared employer with father by age category			
12-17			0.01
			(0.20)
18-19			0.21
			(3.12)
20-21			0.10
			(1.26)
22-23			0.03
			(0.35)
24-25			0.03
			(0.33)
26-30			-0.06
			-(0.55)
31-45			0.15
			(1.49)
Observations (job-years)	222,585	222,585	222,585
Groups (persons)	8,457	8,457	8,457

Dependent variable is the natural log of the daughters' earnings. All regressions include dummy variables for calendar year and daughter's age as well as measures of job tenure and total experience. t-statistics (in parentheses) are calculated with heteroskedasticity-robust standard errors.

Table 14A

Regressions of Sons' Earnings on Shared Employers by Fathers' Earnings Quartile

	(1)	(2)
Shared employer with father		
All	0.23	
	(6.66)	
1st quartile of earnings		-0.04
		-(0.34)
2nd quartile of earnings		0.18
		(2.30)
3rd quartile of earnings		0.30
		(4.99)
4th quartile of earnings		0.29
		(5.31)
Father earnings		
2nd quartile of earnings	0.08	0.08
	(3.23)	(3.10)
3rd quartile of earnings	0.16	0.15
	(6.53)	(6.14)
4th quartile of earnings	0.28	0.28
	(11.32)	(10.88)
Observations (job-years)	252,809	252,809

Dependent variable is the natural log of the sons' earnings. All regressions include dummy variables for calendar year and son's age as well as measures of job tenure and total experience. Father's earnings decile calculated as father's place in the earnings distribution when son was 15. t-statistics (in parentheses) are calculated with heteroskedasticity- and cluster-robust standard errors, with clusters at the son level.

Table 14B

Regressions of daughters' Earnings on Shared Employers by Fathers' Earnings Quartile

	(1)	(2)
Shared employer with father		
All	0.03	
	(0.74)	
1st quartile of earnings		-0.04
		-(0.32)
2nd quartile of earnings		-0.10
		-(0.99)
3rd quartile of earnings		0.03
		(0.30)
4th quartile of earnings		0.13
		(2.04)
Father earnings		
2nd quartile of earnings	0.10	0.10
	(4.25)	(4.29)
3rd quartile of earnings	0.16	0.16
	(7.36)	(7.29)
4th quartile of earnings	0.23	0.22
	(10.32)	(10.10)
Observations (job-years)	222,585	222,585

Dependent variable is the natural log of the daughters' earnings. All regressions include dummy variables for calendar year and daughter's age as well as measures of job tenure and total experience. Father's earnings decile calculated as father's place in the earnings distribution when son was 15. t-statistics (in parentheses) are calculated with heteroskedasticity- and cluster-robust standard errors, with clusters at the daughter level.

Table 15A
Fixed Effects Regressions of Sons' Earnings on Shared Employers with Employer Characteristics

	(1)	(2)
Shared employer with father	0.22	
	(6.71)	
Shared employer with father by firm size		
1-9 empl.		-0.09
		-(1.23)
10-25 empl.		0.07
		(0.91)
26-50 empl.		0.01
		(0.13)
51-100 empl.		0.21
		(2.55)
101-200 empl.		0.10
		(0.96)
201-500 empl.		0.34
		(3.61)
501-1000 empl.		0.39
		(3.17)
1000+ empl.		0.51
		(8.79)
firm size missing		0.10
		(0.61)
Observations (job-years)	252,809	252,809
Groups (persons)	9,337	9,337

Dependent variable is the natural log of the sons' earnings. All regressions include dummy variables for firm size, firm type, calendar year, and son's age as well as measures of job tenure and total experience. t-statistics (in parentheses) are calculated with heteroskedasticity-robust standard errors.

Table 15B
Fixed Effects Regressions of Daughters' Earnings on Shared Employers with Employer Characteristics

	(1)	(2)
Shared employer with father	0.10	
	(2.03)	
Shared employer with father by firm size		
1-9 empl.		-0.08
		-(0.80)
10-25 empl.		0.06
		(0.44)
26-50 empl.		0.04
		(0.31)
51-100 empl.		0.06
		(0.45)
101-200 empl.		-0.24
		-(1.37)
201-500 empl.		0.09
		(0.61)
501-1000 empl.		-0.23
		-(1.28)
1000+ empl.		0.30
		(4.17)
firm size missing		0.28
		(1.49)
Observations (job-years)	222,585	222,585
Groups (persons)	8,457	8,457

Dependent variable is the natural log of the daughters' earnings. All regressions include dummy variables for firm size, firm type, calendar year, and daughter's age as well as measures of job tenure and total experience. t-statistics (in parentheses) are calculated with heteroskedasticity-robust standard errors.

Table 16A
Fixed Effects Regressions of Sons' Earnings on Shared Employers with Employer Characteristics

	(1)	(2)
Shared employer with father	0.07	
	(2.32)	
Shared employer with father by NAICS sector		
Agriculture, forestry, fishing, and hunting		0.05
		(0.27)
Mining, quarrying, and oil and gas extraction		0.16
		(0.74)
Utilities		-0.35
		-(1.10)
Construction		0.12
		(1.48)
Manufacturing		0.08
		(1.30)
Wholesale trade		-0.24
		-(2.44)
Retail trade		-0.04
		-(0.41)
Transportation and warehousing		-0.06
		-(0.28)
Information		0.13
		(0.30)
Finance and insurance		0.17
		(0.79)
Real estate and rental and leasing		-0.11
		-(0.41)
Professional, scientific, and technical services		0.12
		(0.95)
Management of companies and enterprises		0.82
		(1.15)
Administrative support and waste management		0.58
		(3.76)
Education services		0.26
		(1.87)
Health care and social assistance		0.05
		(0.30)
Arts, entertainment, and recreation		-0.72
		-(2.60)
Accommodation and food services		0.37
		(2.37)
Other services		-0.14
		-(0.82)
Public sector		-0.02
		-(0.10)
Government		0.21
		(1.04)
Sector information missing		0.43
		(2.44)
Observations (job-years)	252,809	252,809
Groups (persons)	9,337	9,337

Dependent variable is the natural log of the sons' earnings. All regressions include dummy variables for firm size, firm type, employer sector, calendar year, and son's age as well as measures of job tenure and total experience. t-statistics (in parentheses) are calculated with heteroskedasticity-robust standard errors.

Table 16B
Fixed Effects Regressions of Daughters' Earnings on Shared Employers with Employer Characteristics

	(1)	(2)
Shared employer with father	-0.07	
	-(1.52)	
Shared employer with father by NAICS sector		
Agriculture, forestry, fishing, and hunting		0.15
		(0.41)
Mining, quarrying, and oil and gas extraction		-0.12
		-(0.30)
Utilities		-0.26
		-(1.20)
Construction		-0.03
		-(0.12)
Manufacturing		0.02
		(0.15)
Wholesale trade		-0.17
		-(1.22)
Retail trade		0.16
		(1.26)
Transportation and warehousing		-0.18
		-(0.60)
Information		-0.76
		-(2.11)
Finance and insurance		-0.12
		-(0.57)
Real estate and rental and leasing		0.16
		(0.58)
Professional, scientific, and technical services		-0.43
		-(2.76)
Management of companies and enterprises		0.91
		(1.62)
Administrative support and waste management		0.44
		(1.99)
Education services		-0.24
		-(1.33)
Health care and social assistance		-0.48
		-(3.14)
Arts, entertainment, and recreation		-0.16
		-(0.96)
Accommodation and food services		0.19
		(1.24)
Other services		0.23
		(0.96)
Public sector		-0.14
		-(0.53)
Government		0.07
		(0.40)
Sector information missing		-0.31
		-(1.02)
Observations (job-years)	222,585	222,585
Groups (persons)	8,457	8,457

Dependent variable is the natural log of the daughters' earnings. All regressions include dummy variables for firm size, firm type, employer sector, calendar year, and daughter's age as well as measures of job tenure and total experience. t-statistics (in parentheses) are calculated with heteroskedasticity-robust standard errors.

Table 17A
Regressions of Sons' Earnings on Shared Employers for Specific jobs

	First job		Highest-paying job at age 30	
	(1)	(2)	(3)	(4)
Shared employer with father	0.24	0.23	0.13	0.10
	(4.52)	(4.19)	(2.21)	(1.64)
Firm characteristics included	No	Yes	No	Yes
Observations (job-years)	9,121	9,121	7,677	7,677

Dependent variable is the natural log of the sons' earnings. All regressions include dummy variables for calendar year and son's age as well as measures of job tenure and total experience. t-statistics (in parentheses) are calculated with heteroskedasticity- and cluster-robust standard errors, with clusters at the son level.
Columns 1 and 2 include only jobs at the sons' first employers.
Columns 3 and 4 include only the jobs with the highest earnings at age 30.

Table 17B
Regressions of Daughters' Earnings on Shared Employers for Specific jobs

	First job		Highest-paying job at age 30	
	(1)	(2)	(3)	(4)
Shared employer with father	0.05	0.12	-0.02	-0.05
	(0.72)	(1.56)	-(0.16)	-(0.47)
Firm characteristics included	No	Yes	No	Yes
Observations (job-years)	8,318	8,318	6,725	6,725

Dependent variable is the natural log of the daughters' earnings. All regressions include dummy variables for calendar year and daughter's age as well as measures of job tenure and total experience. t-statistics (in parentheses) are calculated with heteroskedasticity- and cluster-robust standard errors, with clusters at the dadughter level.
Columns 1 and 2 include only jobs at the daughters' first employers.
Columns 3 and 4 include only the jobs with the highest earnings at age 30.

www.ingramcontent.com/pod-product-compliance
Lightning Source LLC
Chambersburg PA
CBHW081758170526

45167CB00008B/3234